Ashtavakra Gita

Ashtavakra Gita

The Heart of Awareness

A bilingual edition in Sanskrit and English

Attributed to
Ashtavakra

Transcribed and translated by
John Richards

evertype
2019

Published by Evertype, 19A Corso Street, Dundee, DD2 1DR, Scotland. www.evertype.com.

Editor: Michael Everson.

A catalogue record for this book is available from the British Library.

ISBN-10 1-78201-261-3
ISBN-13 978-1-78201-261-0

Typeset in Baskerville and New Pelican by Michael Everson.

Design and cover design: Michael Everson. "Circle Floral design" © Krishna Kharidehal, www.dreamstime.com/krishnasomya_info.

Preface

I first encountered the *Ashtavakra Gita* when Gabriel Rosenstock offered me his poetic translation into Irish of it. We decided to publish it in a bilingual Sanskrit and Irish edition,[1] and it was in seeking out the Sanskrit text that I found both John Richards' transcription and his English translation of it.

The Reverend John Henry Richards, MA, BD, was an Anglican priest born in 1934 who was ordained a deacon in Llandaff in 1977 and a priest there in 1978. He served in Maesteg, Cardiff, Penmark, and Stackpile Elidor until his retirement in 1999, and died in 2017. He is known for his English translations of the *Ashtavakra Gita*, the *Dhammapada*, and the *Vivekachudamani*, which he put in the public domain and distributed on the Internet in 1994. The text used here is the one revised in 1996.

I have made a very few alterations to John's text and translation, replacing the Devanagari daṇḍa and double daṇḍa with the vertical bar and double vertical bar surrounding the verse numbers in the Sanskrit text, adding "said" to correspond to *uvāca* to introduce the dialogue in the translation, and favouring Oxford spelling.

Michael Everson
Dundee, December 2019

1 Gabriel Rosenstock, tr. 2019. *Ashtávakra Gítá - Aṣṭāvakra Gītā: Eagrán dátheangach i Sanscrait agus i nGaeilge*. Dundee: Evertype. ISBN 978-1-78201-257-3.

Introduction

The *Ashtavakra Gita*, or the *Ashtavakra Samhita* as it is sometimes called, is a very ancient Sanskrit text. Nothing seems to be known about the author, though tradition ascribes it to the sage Ashtavakra; hence the name.

There is little doubt though that it is very old, probably dating back to the days of the classic Vedanta period. The Sanskrit style and the doctrine expressed would seem to warrant this assessment.

The work was known, appreciated and quoted by Ramakrishna and his disciple Vivekananda, as well as by Ramana Maharshi, while Radhakrishnan always refers to it with great respect. Apart from that the work speaks for itself. It presents the traditional teachings of Advaita Vedanta with a clarity and power very rarely matched.

The translation here is by John Richards, and is presented to the public domain with his affection. The work has been a constant inspiration in his life for many years. May it be so for many others.

John Richards
Stackpole Elidor, Wales, May 1994

Ashtavakra Gita

Anukramaṇikā

1 Sākṣi . . . 4
2 Āścaryam . . . 10
3 Ātmādvaita . . . 18
4 Sarvamātmā . . . 22
5 Laya . . . 24
6 Prakṛteḥ Paraḥ . . . 26
7 Śānta . . . 28
8 Mokṣa . . . 30
9 Nirveda . . . 32
10 Vairāgya . . . 36
11 Cidrupa . . . 40
12 Svabhāva . . . 44
13 Yathāsukham . . . 48
14 Īśvara . . . 52
15 Tattvam . . . 54
16 Svāsthya . . . 60
17 Kaivalya . . . 64
18 Jīvanmukti . . . 70
19 Svamahimā . . . 96
20 Akiñcanabhava . . . 100

Table of Contents

1 Instruction on Self-Realization 5
2 Joy of Self-Realization 11
3 Test of Self-Realization 19
4 Glory of Self-Realization 23
5 Four Ways to Dissolution 25
6 The Higher Knowledge 27
7 Nature of Self-Realization 29
8 Bondage and Liberation 31
9 Detachment 33
10 Quietude 37
11 Wisdom 41
12 Abiding in the Self 45
13 Happiness 49
14 Tranquillity 53
15 Knowledge of the Self 55
16 Special Instruction 61
17 The True Knower 65
18 Peace 71
19 Repose in the Self 97
20 Liberation-in-Life 101

1
Sākṣi

Janaka uvāca ||

kathaṃ jñānamavāpnoti kathaṃ muktirbhaviṣyati |
vairāgyaṃ ca kathaṃ prāptaṃ etad brūhi mama prabho || 1-1 ||

Aṣṭāvakra uvāca ||

muktiṃ icchasi cettāta viṣayān viṣavattyaja |
kṣamārjavadayātoṣasatyaṃ pīyūṣavad bhaja || 1-2 ||

na pṛthvī na jalaṃ nāgnirna vāyurdyaurna vā bhavān |
eṣāṃ sākṣiṇamātmānaṃ cidrūpaṃ viddhi muktaye || 1-3 ||

yadi dehaṃ pṛthak kṛtya citi viśrāmya tiṣṭhasi |
adhunaiva sukhī śānto bandhamukto bhaviṣyasi || 1-4 ||

na tvaṃ viprādiko varṇo nāśramī nākṣagocaraḥ |
asaṅgo'si nirākāro viśvasākṣī sukhī bhava || 1-5 ||

1

Instruction on Self-Realization

Janaka said:

1.1 How is knowledge to be acquired? How is liberation to be attained? And how is dispassion to be reached? Tell me this, sir.

Aṣṭāvakra said:

1.2 If you are seeking liberation, my son, shun the objects of the senses like poison. Practise tolerance, sincerity, compassion, contentment and truthfulness like nectar.

1.3 You are neither earth, water, fire, air or even ether. For liberation know yourself as consisting of consciousness, the witness of these.

1.4 If only you will remain resting in consciousness, seeing yourself as distinct from the body, then even now you will become happy, peaceful and free from bonds.

1.5 You do not belong to the brahmin or any other caste, you are not at any stage, nor are you anything that the eye can see. You are unattached and formless, the witness of everything—so be happy.

dharmādharmau sukhaṃ duḥkhaṃ mānasāni na te vibho |
na kartāsi na bhoktāsi mukta evāsi sarvadā || 1-6 ||

eko draṣṭāsi sarvasya muktaprāyo'si sarvadā |
ayameva hi te bandho draṣṭāraṃ paśyasītaram || 1-7 ||

ahaṃ kartetyahaṃmānamahākṛṣṇāhidaṃśitaḥ |
nāhaṃ karteti viśvāsāmṛtaṃ pītvā sukhī bhava || 1-8 ||

eko viśuddhabodho'haṃ iti niścayavahninā |
prajvālyājñānagahanaṃ vītaśokaḥ sukhī bhava || 1-9 ||

yatra viśvamidaṃ bhāti kalpitaṃ rajjusarpavat |
ānandaparamānandaḥ sa bodhastvaṃ sukhaṃ bhava || 1-10 ||

muktābhimānī mukto hi baddho baddhābhimānyapi |
kiṃvadantīha satyeyaṃ yā matiḥ sā gatirbhavet || 1-11 ||

ātmā sākṣī vibhuḥ pūrṇa eko muktaścidakriyaḥ |
asaṃgo niḥspṛhaḥ śānto bhramātsaṃsāravāniva || 1-12 ||

kūṭasthaṃ bodhamadvaitamātmānaṃ paribhāvaya |
ābhāso'haṃ bhramaṃ muktvā bhāvaṃ bāhyamathāntaram || 1-13 ||

1.6 Righteousness and unrighteousness, pleasure and pain are purely of the mind and are no concern of yours. You are neither the doer nor the reaper of the consequences, so you are always free.

1.7 You are the one witness of everything, and are always totally free. The cause of your bondage is that you see the witness as something other than this.

1.8 Since you have been bitten by the black snake of the self-opinion that “I am the doer”, drink the nectar of faith in the fact that “I am not the doer”, and be happy.

1.9 Burn down the forest of ignorance with the fire of the understanding that “I am the one pure awareness”, and be happy and free from distress.

1.10 That in which all this appears—imagined like the snake in a rope, that joy, supreme joy and awareness is what you are, so be happy.

1.11 If one thinks of oneself as free, one is free, and if one thinks of oneself as bound, one is bound. Here this saying is true, "Thinking makes it so".

1.12 Your real nature is as the one perfect, free, and actionless consciousness, the all-pervading witness—unattached to anything, desireless and at peace. It is from illusion that you seem to be involved in samsara.

1.13 Meditate on yourself as motionless awareness, free from any dualism, giving up the mistaken idea that you are just a derivative consciousness, or anything external or internal.

dehābhimānapāśena ciraṃ baddho'si putraka |
bodho'haṃ jñānakhaṃgena tannikṛtya sukhī bhava || 1-14 ||

niḥsaṃgo niṣkriyo'si tvaṃ svaprakāśo niraṃjanaḥ |
ayameva hi te bandhaḥ samādhimanutiṣṭhati || 1-15 ||

tvayā vyāptamidaṃ viśvaṃ tvayi protaṃ yathārthataḥ |
śuddhabuddhasvarūpastvaṃ mā gamaḥ kṣudracittatām || 1-16 ||

nirapekṣo nirvikāro nirbharaḥ śītalāśayaḥ |
agādhabuddhirakṣubdho bhava cinmātravāsanaḥ || 1-17 ||

sākāramanṛtaṃ viddhi nirākāraṃ tu niścalam |
etattattvopadeśena na punarbhavasambhavaḥ || 1-18 ||

yathaivādarśamadhyasthe rūpe'ntaḥ paritastu saḥ |
tathaivā'smin śarīre'ntaḥ paritaḥ parameśvaraḥ || 1-19 ||

ekaṃ sarvagataṃ vyoma bahirantaryathā ghaṭe |
nityaṃ nirantaraṃ brahma sarvabhūtagaṇe tathā || 1-20 ||

1.14 You have long been trapped in the snare of identification with the body. Sever it with the knife of knowledge that "I am awareness", and be happy, my son.

1.15 You are really unbound and actionless, self-illuminating and spotless already. The cause of your bondage is that you are still resorting to stilling the mind.

1.16 All of this is really filled by you and strung out in you, for what you consist of is pure awareness—so don't be small minded.

1.17 You are unconditioned and changeless, formless and immovable, unfathomable awareness and unperturbable, so hold to nothing but consciousness.

1.18 Recognize that the apparent is unreal, while the unmanifest is abiding. Through this initiation into truth you will escape falling into unreality again.

1.19 Just as a mirror exists everywhere both within and apart from its reflected images, so the Supreme Lord exists everywhere within and apart from this body.

1.20 Just as one and the same all-pervading space exists within and without a jar, so the eternal, everlasting God exists in the totality of things.

2

Āścaryam

Janaka uvāca ||

aho niraṃjanaḥ śānto bodho'haṃ prakṛteḥ paraḥ |
etāvantamahaṃ kālaṃ mohenaiva viḍambitaḥ || 2-1 ||

yathā prakāśayāmyeko dehamenaṃ tathā jagat |
ato mama jagatsarvamathavā na ca kiṃcana || 2-2 ||

sa śarīramaho viśvaṃ parityajya mayādhunā |
kutaścit kauśalād eva paramātmā vilokyate || 2-3 ||

yathā na toyato bhinnāstaraṃgāḥ phenabudbudāḥ |
ātmano na tathā bhinnaṃ viśvamātmavinirgatam || 2-4 ||

tantumātro bhaved eva paṭo yadvad vicāritaḥ |
ātmatanmātramevedaṃ tadvad viśvaṃ vicāritam || 2-5 ||

yathaivekṣurase klṛptā tena vyāptaiva śarkarā |
tathā viśvaṃ mayi klṛptaṃ mayā vyāptaṃ nirantaram || 2-6 ||

2

Joy of Self-Realization

Janaka said:

2.1 Truly I am spotless and at peace, the awareness beyond natural causality. All this time I have been afflicted by delusion.

2.2 As I alone give light to this body, so I do to the world, As a result the whole world is mine, or alternatively nothing is.

2.3 So now abandoning the body and everything else, by some good fortune or other my true self becomes apparent.

2.4 Just as waves, foam and bubbles are not different from water, so all this which has emanated from oneself, is no other than oneself.

2.5 In the same way that cloth is found to be just thread when analysed, so when all this is analysed it is found to be no other than oneself.

2.6 Just as the sugar produced from the juice of the sugarcane is permeated with the same taste, so all this, produced out of me, is completely permeated with me.

ātmajñānājjagad bhāti ātmajñānānna bhāsate |
rajjvajñānādahirbhāti tajjñānād bhāsate na hi || 2-7 ||

prakāśo me nijaṃ rūpaṃ nātirikto'smyahaṃ tataḥ |
yadā prakāśate viśvaṃ tadāhaṃ bhāsa eva hi || 2-8 ||

aho vikalpitaṃ viśvamajñānānmayi bhāsate |
rūpyaṃ śuktau phaṇī rajjau vāri sūryakare yathā || 2-9 ||

matto vinirgataṃ viśvaṃ mayyeva layameṣyati |
mṛdi kumbho jale vīciḥ kanake kaṭakaṃ yathā || 2-10 ||

aho ahaṃ namo mahyaṃ vināśo yasya nāsti me |
brahmādistambaparyantaṃ jagannāśo'pi tiṣṭhataḥ || 2-11 ||

aho ahaṃ namo mahyaṃ eko'haṃ dehavānapi |
kvacinna gantā nāgantā vyāpya viśvamavasthitaḥ || 2-12 ||

aho ahaṃ namo mahyaṃ dakṣo nāstīha matsamaḥ |
asaṃspṛśya śarīreṇa yena viśvaṃ ciraṃ dhṛtam || 2-13 ||

aho ahaṃ namo mahyaṃ yasya me nāsti kiṃcana |
athavā yasya me sarvaṃ yad vāṅmanasagocaram || 2-14 ||

2.7 From ignorance of oneself, the world appears, and by knowledge of oneself it appears no longer. From ignorance of the rope a snake appears, and by knowledge of it, it appears no longer.

2.8 Shining is my essential nature, and I am nothing over and beyond that. When the world shines forth, it is simply me that is shining forth.

2.9 All this appears in me imagined due to ignorance, just as a snake appears in the rope, the mirage of water in the sunlight, and silver in mother of pearl.

2.10 All this, which has originated out of me, is resolved back into me too, like a jug back into clay, a wave into water, and a bracelet into gold.

2.11 How wonderful I am! Glory be to me, for whom there is no destruction, remaining even beyond the destruction of the world from Brahma down to the last clump of grass.

2.12 How wonderful I am! Glory be to me, solitary even though with a body, neither going or coming anywhere, I who abide forever, filling all that is.

2.13 How wonderful I am! Glory be to me! There is no one so clever as me! I who have borne all that is forever, without even touching it with my body!

2.14 How wonderful I am! Glory be to me! I who possess nothing at all, or alternatively possess everything that speech and mind can refer to.

jñānaṃ jñeyaṃ tathā jñātā tritayaṃ nāsti vāstavam |
ajñānād bhāti yatredaṃ so'hamasmi niraṃjanaḥ || 2-15 ||

dvaitamūlamaho duḥkhaṃ nānyattasyā'sti bheṣajam |
dṛśyametan mṛṣā sarvaṃ eko'haṃ cidrasomalaḥ || 2-16 ||

bodhamātro'hamajñānād upādhiḥ kalpito mayā |
evaṃ vimṛśato nityaṃ nirvikalpe sthitirmama || 2-17 ||

na me bandho'sti mokṣo vā bhrāntiḥ śānto nirāśrayā |
aho mayi sthitaṃ viśvaṃ vastuto na mayi sthitam || 2-18 ||

saśarīramidaṃ viśvaṃ na kiṃciditi niścitam |
śuddhacinmātra ātmā ca tatkasmin kalpanādhunā || 2-19 ||

śarīraṃ svarganarakau bandhamokṣau bhayaṃ tathā |
kalpanāmātramevaitat kiṃ me kāryaṃ cidātmanaḥ || 2-20 ||

aho janasamūhe'pi na dvaitaṃ paśyato mama |
araṇyamiva saṃvṛttaṃ kva ratiṃ karavāṇyaham || 2-21 ||

nāhaṃ deho na me deho jīvo nāhamahaṃ hi cit |
ayameva hi me bandha āsīdyā jīvite spṛhā || 2-22 ||

2.15 Knowledge, what is to be known, and the knower—these three do not exist in reality. I am the spotless reality in which they appear because of ignorance.

2.16 Truly dualism is the root of suffering. There is no other remedy for it than the realization that all this that we see is unreal, and that I am the one stainless reality, consisting of consciousness.

2.17 I am pure awareness though through ignorance I have imagined myself to have additional attributes. By continually reflecting like this, my dwelling place is in the Unimagined.

2.18 For me there is neither bondage nor liberation. The illusion has lost its basis and ceased. Truly all this exists in me, though ultimately it does not even exist in me.

2.19 I have recognized that all this and my body are nothing, While my true self is nothing but pure consciousness, so what can the imagination work on now?

2.20 The body, heaven and hell, bondage and liberation, and fear too, All this is pure imagination. What is there left to do for me whose very nature is consciousness?

2.21 Truly I do not see dualism even in a crowd of people. What pleasure should I have when it has turned into a wilderness?

2.22 I am not the body, nor is the body mine. I am not a living being. I am consciousness. It was my thirst for living that was my bondage.

aho bhuvanakallolairvicitrairdrāk samutthitam |
mayyanaṃtamahāmbhodhau cittavāte samudyate || 2-23 ||

mayyanaṃtamahāmbhodhau cittavāte praśāmyati |
abhāgyājjīvavaṇijo jagatpoto vinaśvaraḥ || 2-24 ||

mayyanantamahāmbhodhāvāścaryaṃ jīvavīcayaḥ |
udyanti ghnanti khelanti praviśanti svabhāvataḥ || 2-25 ||

2.23 Truly it is in the limitless ocean of myself, that stimulated by the colourful waves of the worlds everything suddenly arises in the wind of consciousness.

2.24 It is in the limitless ocean of myself, that the wind of thought subsides, and the trader-like living beings' world bark is wrecked by lack of goods.

2.25 How wonderful it is that in the limitless ocean of myself the waves of living beings arise, collide, play and disappear, according to their natures.

3

Ātmādvaita

Aṣṭāvakra uvāca ||

avināśinamātmānaṃ ekaṃ vijñāya tattvataḥ |
tavātmajñānasya dhīrasya kathamarthārjane ratiḥ || 3-1 ||

ātmājñānādaho prītirviṣayabhramagocare |
śukterajñānato lobho yathā rajatavibhrame || 3-2 ||

viśvaṃ sphurati yatredaṃ taraṅgā iva sāgare |
so'hamasmīti vijñāya kiṃ dīna iva dhāvasi || 3-3 ||

śrutvāpi śuddhacaitanya ātmānamatisundaram |
upasthe'tyantasaṃsakto mālinyamadhigacchati || 3-4 ||

sarvabhūteṣu cātmānaṃ sarvabhūtāni cātmani |
munerjānata āścaryaṃ mamatvamanuvartate || 3-5 ||

āsthitaḥ paramādvaitaṃ mokṣārthe'pi vyavasthitaḥ |
āścaryaṃ kāmavaśago vikalaḥ keliśikṣayā || 3-6 ||

3

Test of Self-Realization

Aṣṭāvakra said:

3.1 Knowing yourself as truly one and indestructible, how could a wise man possessing self-knowledge like you feel any pleasure in acquiring wealth?

3.2 Truly, when one does not know oneself, one takes pleasure in the objects of mistaken perception, just as greed arises for the mistaken silver in one who does not know mother of pearl for what it is.

3.3 All this wells up like waves in the sea. Recognizing, "I am That", why run around like someone in need?

3.4 After hearing of oneself as pure consciousness and the supremely beautiful, is one to go on lusting after sordid sexual objects?

3.5 When the sage has realized that he himself is in all beings, and all beings are in him, it is astonishing that the sense of individuality should be able to continue.

3.6 It is astonishing that a man who has reached the supreme non-dual state and is intent on the benefits of liberation should still be subject to lust and held back by sexual activity.

udbhūtaṃ jñānadurmitramavadhāryātidurbalaḥ |
āścaryaṃ kāmamākāṅkṣet kālamantamanuśritaḥ || 3-7 ||

ihāmutra viraktasya nityānityavivekinaḥ |
āścaryaṃ mokṣakāmasya mokṣād eva vibhīṣikā || 3-8 ||

dhīrastu bhojyamāno'pi pīḍyamāno'pi sarvadā |
ātmānaṃ kevalaṃ paśyan na tuṣyati na kupyati || 3-9 ||

ceṣṭamānaṃ śarīraṃ svaṃ paśyatyanyaśarīravat |
saṃstave cāpi nindāyāṃ kathaṃ kṣubhyet mahāśayaḥ || 3-10 ||

māyāmātramidaṃ viśvaṃ paśyan vigatakautukaḥ |
api sannihite mṛtyau kathaṃ trasyati dhīradhīḥ || 3-11 ||

niḥspṛhaṃ mānasaṃ yasya nairāśye'pi mahātmanaḥ |
tasyātmajñānatṛptasya tulanā kena jāyate || 3-12 ||

svabhāvād eva jānāno dṛśyametanna kiṃcana |
idaṃ grāhyamidaṃ tyājyaṃ sa kiṃ paśyati dhīradhīḥ || 3-13 ||

aṃtastyaktakaṣāyasya nirdvandvasya nirāśiṣaḥ |
yadṛcchayāgato bhogo na duḥkhāya na tuṣṭaye || 3-14 ||

3.7 It is astonishing that one already very debilitated, and knowing very well that its arousal is the enemy of knowledge should still hanker after sensuality, even when approaching his last days.

3.8 It is astonishing that one who is unattached to the things of this world or the next, who discriminates between the permanent and the impermanent, and who longs for liberation, should still feel fear for liberation.

3.9 Whether feted or tormented, the wise man is always aware of his supreme self-nature and is neither pleased nor disappointed.

3.10 The great souled person sees even his own body in action as if it were some-one else's, so how should he be disturbed by praise or blame?

3.11 Seeing this world as pure illusion, and devoid of any interest in it, how should the strong-minded person, feel fear, even at the approach of death?

3.12 Who is to be compared to the great souled person whose mind is free of desire even in disappointment, and who has found satisfaction in self-knowledge?

3.13 How should a strong-minded person, who knows that what he sees is by its very nature nothing, consider one thing to be grasped and another to be rejected?

3.14 For someone who has eliminated attachment, and who is free from dualism and from desire, an object of enjoyment that comes of itself is neither painful nor pleasurable.

4

Sarvamātmā

Janaka uvāca ||

hantātmajñānasya dhīrasya khelato bhogalīlayā |
na hi saṃsāravāhīkairmūḍhaiḥ saha samānatā || 4-1 ||

yat padaṃ prepsavo dīnāḥ śakrādyāḥ sarvadevatāḥ |
aho tatra sthito yogī na harṣamupagacchati || 4-2 ||

tajjñasya puṇyapāpābhyāṃ sparśo hyantarna jāyate |
na hyākāśasya dhūmena dṛśyamānāpi saṅgatiḥ || 4-3 ||

ātmaivedaṃ jagatsarvaṃ jñātaṃ yena mahātmanā |
yadṛcchayā vartamānaṃ taṃ niṣeddhuṃ kṣameta kaḥ || 4-4 ||

ābrahmastambaparyante bhūtagrāme caturvidhe |
vijñasyaiva hi sāmarthyamicchānicchāvivarjane || 4-5 ||

ātmānamadvayaṃ kaścijjānāti jagadīśvaram |
yad vetti tatsa kurute na bhayaṃ tasya kutracit || 4-6 ||

4
Glory of Self-Realization

Janaka said:

4.1 Certainly the wise person of self-knowledge, playing the game of worldly enjoyment, bears no resemblance whatever to the world's bewildered beasts of burden.

4.2 Truly the yogi feels no excitement even at being established in that state which all the Devas from Indra down yearn for disconsolately.

4.3 He who has known That is untouched within by good deeds or bad, just as the sky is not touched by smoke, however much it may appear to be.

4.4 Who can prevent the great-souled person who has known this whole world as himself from living as he pleases?

4.5 Of all four categories of beings, from Brahma down to the last clump of grass, only the man of knowledge is capable of eliminating desire and aversion.

4.6 Rare is the man who knows himself as the undivided Lord of the world, and no fear occurs to him who knows this from anything.

5

Laya

Aṣṭāvakra uvāca ||

na te saṃgo'sti kenāpi kiṃ śuddhastyaktumicchasi |
saṃghātavilayaṃ kurvannevameva layaṃ vraja || 5-1 ||

udeti bhavato viśvaṃ vāridheriva budbudaḥ |
iti jñātvaikamātmānaṃ evameva layaṃ vraja || 5-2 ||

pratyakṣamapyavastutvād viśvaṃ nāstyamale tvayi |
rajjusarpa iva vyaktaṃ evameva layaṃ vraja || 5-3 ||

samaduḥkhasukhaḥ pūrṇa āśānairāśyayoḥ samaḥ |
samajīvitamṛtyuḥ sannevameva layaṃ vraja || 5-4 ||

5
Four Ways to Dissolution

Aṣṭāvakra said:

5.1 You are not bound by anything. What does a pure person like you need to renounce? Putting the complex organism to rest, you can go to your rest.

5.2 All this arises out of you, like a bubble out of the sea. Knowing yourself like this to be but one, you can go to your rest.

5.3 In spite of being in front of your eyes, all this, being insubstantial, does not exist in you, spotless as you are. It is an appearance like the snake in a rope, so you can go to your rest.

5.4 Equal in pain and in pleasure, equal in hope and in disappointment, equal in life and in death, and complete as you are, you can go to your rest.

6

Prakṛtaḥ Paraḥ

Janaka uvāca ||

ākāśavadananto'haṃ ghaṭavat prākṛtaṃ jagat |
iti jñānaṃ tathaitasya na tyāgo na graho layaḥ || 6-1 ||

mahodadhirivāhaṃ sa prapaṃco vīcisa'nnibhaḥ |
iti jñānaṃ tathaitasya na tyāgo na graho layaḥ || 6-2 ||

ahaṃ sa śuktisaṅkāśo rūpyavad viśvakalpanā |
iti jñānaṃ tathaitasya na tyāgo na graho layaḥ || 6-3 ||

ahaṃ vā sarvabhūteṣu sarvabhūtānyatho mayi |
iti jñānaṃ tathaitasya na tyāgo na graho layaḥ || 6-4 ||

6
The Higher Knowledge

Janaka said:

6.1 I am infinite like space, and the natural world is like a jar. To know this is knowledge, and then there is neither renunciation, acceptance or cessation of it.

6.2 I am like the ocean, and the multiplicity of objects is comparable to a wave. To know this is knowledge, and then there is neither renunciation, acceptance or cessation of it.

6.3 I am like the mother of pearl, and the imagined world is like the silver. To know this is knowledge, and then there is neither renunciation, acceptance or cessation of it.

6.4 Alternatively, I am in all beings, and all beings are in me. To know this is knowledge, and then there is neither renunciation, acceptance or cessation of it.

7

Śānta

Janaka uvāca ||

mayyanaṃtamahāmbhodhau viśvapota itastataḥ |
bhramati svāṃtavātena na mamāstyasahiṣṇutā || 7-1 ||

mayyanaṃtamahāmbhodhau jagadvīciḥ svabhāvataḥ |
udetu vāstamāyātu na me vṛddhirna ca kṣatiḥ || 7-2 ||

mayyanaṃtamahāmbhodhau viśvaṃ nāma vikalpanā |
atiśāṃto nirākāra etadevāhamāsthitaḥ || 7-3 ||

nātmā bhāveṣu no bhāvastatrānante niraṃjane |
ityasakto'spṛhaḥ śānta etadevāhamāstitaḥ || 7-4 ||

aho cinmātramevāhaṃ indrajālopamaṃ jagat |
iti mama kathaṃ kutra heyopādeyakalpanā || 7-5 ||

7
Nature of Self-Realization

Janaka said:

7.1 1 It is in the infinite ocean of myself that the world bark wanders here and there, driven by its own inner wind. I am not upset by that.

7.2 Let the world wave rise or vanish of its own nature in the infinite ocean of myself. There is no increase or diminution to me from it.

7.3 It is in the infinite ocean of myself that the imagination called the world takes place. I am supremely peaceful and formless, and as such I remain.

7.4 My true nature is not contained in objects, nor does any object exist in it, for it is infinite and spotless. So it is unattached, desireless and at peace, and as such I remain.

7.5 Truly I am but pure consciousness, and the world is like a conjuror's show, so how could I imagine there is anything there to take up or reject?

8

Mokṣa

Aṣṭāvakra uvāca ||

tadā bandho yadā cittaṃ kiñcid vāñchati śocati |
kiṃcin muṃcati gṛṇhāti kiṃcid dṛṣyati kupyati || 8-1 ||

tadā muktiryadā cittaṃ na vāñchati na śocati |
na muṃcati na gṛṇhāti na hṛṣyati na kupyati || 8-2 ||

tadā bandho yadā cittaṃ saktaṃ kāśvapi dṛṣṭiṣu |
tadā mokṣo yadā cittamasaktaṃ sarvadṛṣṭiṣu || 8-3 ||

yadā nāhaṃ tadā mokṣo yadāhaṃ bandhanaṃ tadā |
matveti helayā kiṃcinmā gṛhāṇa vimuṃca mā || 8-4 ||

8
Bondage and Liberation

Aṣṭāvakra said:

8.1 Bondage is when the mind longs for something, grieves about something, rejects something, holds on to something, is pleased about something or displeased about something.

8.2 Liberation is when the mind does not long for anything, grieve about anything, reject anything, or hold on to anything, and is not pleased about anything or displeased about anything.

8.3 Bondage is when the mind is tangled in one of the senses, and liberation is when the mind is not tangled in any of the senses.

8.4 When there is no "me" that is liberation, and when there is "me" there is bondage. Considering this earnestly, do not hold on and do not reject.

9
Nirveda

Aṣṭāvakra uvāca ||

kṛtākṛte ca dvandvāni kadā śāntāni kasya vā |
evaṃ jñātveha nirvedād bhava tyāgaparo'vratī || 9-1 ||

kasyāpi tāta dhanyasya lokaceṣṭāvalokanāt |
jīvitecchā bubhukṣā ca bubhutsopaśamaḥ gatāḥ || 9-2 ||

anityaṃ sarvamevedaṃ tāpatritayadūṣitam |
asāraṃ ninditaṃ heyamiti niścitya śāmyati || 9-3 ||

ko'sau kālo vayaḥ kiṃ vā yatra dvandvāni no nṛṇām |
tānyupekṣya yathāprāptavartī siddhimavāpnuyāt || 9-4 ||

nānā mataṃ maharṣīṇāṃ sādhūnāṃ yogināṃ tathā |
dṛṣṭvā nirvedamāpannaḥ ko na śāmyati mānavaḥ || 9-5 ||

9
Detachment

Aṣṭāvakra said:

9.1 Knowing when the dualism of things done and undone has been put to rest, or the person for whom they occur has, then you can here and now go beyond renunciation and obligations by indifference to such things.

9.2 Rare indeed, my son, is the lucky man whose observation of the world's behaviour has led to the extinction of his thirst for living, thirst for pleasure and thirst for knowledge.

9.3 All this is impermanent and spoilt by the three sorts of pain. Recognizing it to be insubstantial, contemptible and only fit for rejection, one attains peace.

9.4 When was that age or time of life when the dualism of extremes did not exist for men? Abandoning them, a person who is happy to take whatever comes attains perfection.

9.5 Who does not end up with indifference to such things and attain peace when he has seen the differences of opinions among the great sages, saints and yogis?

kṛtvā mūrtiparijñānaṃ caitanyasya na kiṃ guruḥ |
nirvedasamatāyuktyā yastārayati saṃsṛteḥ || 9-6 ||

paśya bhūtavikārāṃstvaṃ bhūtamātrān yathārthataḥ |
tatkṣaṇād bandhanirmuktaḥ svarūpastho bhaviṣyasi || 9-7 ||

vāsanā eva saṃsāra iti sarvā vimuṃca tāḥ |
tattyāgo vāsanātyāgātsthitiradya yathā tathā || 9-8 ||

9.6 Is he not a guru who, endowed with dispassion and equanimity, achieves full knowledge of the nature of consciousness, and leads others out of samsara?

9.7 If you would just see the transformations of the elements as nothing more than the elements, then you would immediately be freed from all bonds and established in your own nature.

9.8 One's inclinations are samsara. Knowing this, abandon them. The renunciation of them is the renunciation of it. Now you can remain as you are.

10

Vairāgya

Aṣṭāvakra uvāca ||

vihāya vairiṇaṃ kāmamarthaṃ cānarthasaṃkulam |
dharmamapyetayorhetuṃ sarvatrānādaraṃ kuru || 10-1 ||

svapnendrajālavat paśya dināni trīṇi paṃca vā |
mitrakṣetradhanāgāradāradāyādisampadaḥ || 10-2 ||

yatra yatra bhavettṛṣṇā saṃsāraṃ viddhi tatra vai |
prauḍhavairāgyamāśritya vītatṛṣṇaḥ sukhī bhava || 10-3 ||

tṛṣṇāmātrātmako bandhastannāśo mokṣa ucyate |
bhavāsaṃsaktimātreṇa prāptituṣṭirmuhurmuhuḥ || 10-4 ||

tvamekaścetanaḥ śuddho jaḍaṃ viśvamasattathā |
avidyāpi na kiṃcitsā kā bubhutsā tathāpi te || 10-5 ||

rājyaṃ sutāḥ kalatrāṇi śarīrāṇi sukhāni ca |
saṃsaktasyāpi naṣṭāni tava janmani janmani || 10-6 ||

10
Quietude

Aṣṭāvakra said:

10.1 Abandoning desire, the enemy, along with gain, itself so full of loss, and the good deeds which are the cause of the other two—practise indifference to everything.

10.2 Look on such things as friends, land, money, property, wife, and bequests as nothing but a dream or a three or five-day conjuror's show.

10.3 Wherever a desire occurs, see samsara in it. Establishing yourself in firm dispassion, be free of passion and happy.

10.4 The essential nature of bondage is nothing other than desire, and its elimination is known as liberation. It is simply by not being attached to changing things that the everlasting joy of attainment is reached.

10.5 You are one, conscious and pure, while all this is just inert non-being. Ignorance itself is nothing, so what need have you of desire to understand?

10.6 Kingdoms, children, wives, bodies, pleasures—these have all been lost to you life after life, attached to them though you were.

alamarthena kāmena sukṛtenāpi karmaṇā |
ebhyaḥ saṃsārakāntāre na viśrāntamabhūn manaḥ || 10-7 ||

kṛtaṃ na kati janmāni kāyena manasā girā |
duḥkhamāyāsadaṃ karma tadadyāpyuparamyatām || 10-8 ||

10.7 Enough of wealth, sensuality and good deeds. In the forest of samsara the mind has never found satisfaction in these.

10.8 How many births have you not done hard and painful labour with body, mind and speech. Now at last stop!

11
Cidrūpa

Aṣṭāvakra uvāca ||

bhāvābhāvavikāraśca svabhāvāditi niścayī |
nirvikāro gatakleśaḥ sukhenaivopaśāmyati || 11-1 ||

īśvaraḥ sarvanirmātā nehānya iti niścayī |
antargalitasarvāśaḥ śāntaḥ kvāpi na sajjate || 11-2 ||

āpadaḥ sampadaḥ kāle daivādeveti niścayī |
tṛptaḥ svasthendriyo nityaṃ na vānchati na śocati || 11-3 ||

sukhaduḥkhe janmamṛtyū daivādeveti niścayī |
sādhyādarśī nirāyāsaḥ kurvannapi na lipyate || 11-4 ||

cintayā jāyate duḥkhaṃ nānyatheheti niścayī |
tayā hīnaḥ sukhī śāntaḥ sarvatra galitaspṛhaḥ || 11-5 ||

11
Wisdom

Aṣṭāvakra said:

11.1 Unmoved and undistressed, realizing that being, non-being and transformation are of the very nature of things, one easily finds peace.

11.2 At peace, having shed all desires within, and realizing that nothing exists here but the Lord, the Creator of all things, one is no longer attached to anything.

11.3 Realizing that misfortune and fortune come in their turn from fate, one is contented, one's senses under control, and does not like or dislike.

11.4 Realizing that pleasure and pain, birth and death are from fate, and that one's desires cannot be achieved, one remains inactive, and even when acting does not get attached.

11.5 Realizing that suffering arises from nothing other than thinking, dropping all desires one rids oneself of it, and is happy and at peace everywhere.

nāhaṃ deho na me deho bodho'hamiti niścayī |
kaivalyaṃ iva samprāpto na smaratyakṛtaṃ kṛtam || 11-6 ||

ābrahmastambaparyantamahameveti niścayī |
nirvikalpaḥ śuciḥ śāntaḥ prāptāprāptavinirvṛtaḥ || 11-7 ||

nāścaryamidaṃ viśvaṃ na kiṃciditi niścayī |
nirvāsanaḥ sphūrtimātro na kiṃcidiva śāmyati || 11-8 ||

11.6 Realizing, "I am not the body, nor is the body mine. I am awareness", one attains the supreme state and no longer remembers things done or undone.

11.7 Realizing, "It is just me, from Brahma down to the last clump of grass", one becomes free from uncertainty, pure, at peace and unconcerned about what has been attained or not.

11.8 Realizing that all this varied and wonderful world is nothing, one becomes pure receptivity, free from inclinations, and as if nothing existed, one finds peace.

12
Svabhāva

Janaka uvāca ||

kāyakṛtyāsahaḥ pūrvaṃ tato vāgvistarāsahaḥ |
atha cintāsahastasmād evamevāhamāsthitaḥ || 12-1 ||

prītyabhāvena śabdāderadṛśyatvena cātmanaḥ |
vikṣepaikāgrahṛdaya evamevāhamāsthitaḥ || 12-2 ||

samādhyāsādivikṣiptau vyavahāraḥ samādhaye |
evaṃ vilokya niyamaṃ evamevāhamāsthitaḥ || 12-3 || |

heyopādeyavirahād evaṃ harṣaviṣādayoḥ |
abhāvādadya he brahmann evamevāhamāsthitaḥ || 12-4 ||

āśramānāśramaṃ dhyānaṃ cittasvīkṛtavarjanam |
vikalpaṃ mama vīkṣyaitairevamevāhamāsthitaḥ || 12-5 ||

karmānuṣṭhānamajñānād yathaivoparamastathā |
budhvā samyagidaṃ tattvaṃ evamevāhamāsthitaḥ || 12-6 ||

12
Abiding in the Self

Janaka said:

12.1 First of all I was averse to physical activity, then to lengthy speech, and finally to thinking itself, which is why I am now established.

12.2 In the absence of delight in sound and the other senses, and by the fact that I am myself not an object of the senses, my mind is focused and free from distraction—which is why I am now established.

12.3 Owing to the distraction of such things as wrong identification, one is driven to strive for mental stillness. Recognizing this pattern I am now established.

12.4 By relinquishing the sense of rejection and acceptance, and with pleasure and disappointment ceasing today, Brahmin, I am now established.

12.5 Life in a community, then going beyond such a state, meditation and the elimination of mind-made objects—by means of these I have seen my error, and I am now established.

12.6 Just as the performance of actions is due to ignorance, so their abandonment is too. By fully recognizing this truth, I am now established.

aciṃtyaṃ ciṃtyamāno'pi cintārūpaṃ bhajatyasau |
tyaktvā tadbhāvanaṃ tasmād evamevāhamāsthitaḥ || 12-7 ||

evameva kṛtaṃ yena sa kṛtārtho bhavedasau |
evameva svabhāvo yaḥ sa kṛtārtho bhavedasau || 12-8 ||

12.7 Trying to think the unthinkable, is doing something unnatural to thought. Abandoning such a practice therefore, I am now established.

12.8 He who has achieved this has achieved the goal of life. He who is of such a nature has done what has to be done.

13
Yathāsukham

Janaka uvāca ||

akiṃcanabhavaṃ svāsthaṃ kaupīnatve'pi durlabham |
tyāgādāne vihāyāsmādahamāse yathāsukham || 13-1 ||

kutrāpi khedaḥ kāyasya jihvā kutrāpi khedyate |
manaḥ kutrāpi tattyaktvā puruṣārthe sthitaḥ sukham || 13-2 ||

kṛtaṃ kimapi naiva syād iti saṃcintya tattvataḥ |
yadā yatkartumāyāti tat kṛtvāse yathāsukham || 13-3 ||

karmanaiṣkarmyanirbandhabhāvā dehasthayoginaḥ |
saṃyogāyogavirahādahamāse yathāsukham || 13-4 ||

arthānarthau na me sthityā gatyā na śayanena vā |
tiṣṭhan gacchan svapan tasmādahamāse yathāsukham || 13-5 ||

svapato nāsti me hāniḥ siddhiryatnavato na vā |
nāśollāsau vihāyāsmadahamāse yathāsukham || 13-6 ||

13
Happiness

Janaka said:

13.1 The inner freedom of having nothing is hard to achieve, even with just a loin-cloth, but I live as I please abandoning both renunciation and acquisition.

13.2 Sometimes one experiences distress because of one's body, sometimes because of one's tongue, and sometimes because of one's mind. Abandoning all of these, I live as I please in the goal of human existence.

13.3 Recognizing that in reality no action is ever committed, I live as I please, just doing what presents itself to be done.

13.4 Yogis who identify themselves with their bodies are insistent on fulfilling and avoiding certain actions, but I live as I please abandoning attachment and rejection.

13.5 No benefit or loss comes to me by standing, walking or lying down, so consequently I live as I please whether standing, walking or sleeping.

13.6 I lose nothing by sleeping and gain nothing by effort, so consequently I live as I please, abandoning loss and success.

sukhādirūpā niyamaṃ bhāveṣvālokya bhūriśaḥ |
śubhāśubhe vihāyāsmādahamāse yathāsukham || 13-7 ||

13.7 Frequently observing the drawbacks of such things as pleasant objects, I live as I please, abandoning the pleasant and unpleasant.

14

Īśvara

Janaka uvāca ||

prakṛtyā śūnyacitto yaḥ pramādād bhāvabhāvanaḥ |
nidrito bodhita iva kṣīṇasaṃsmaraṇo hi saḥ || 14-1 ||

kva dhanāni kva mitrāṇi kva me viṣayadasyavaḥ |
kva śāstraṃ kva ca vijñānaṃ yadā me galitā spṛhā || 14-2 ||

vijñāte sākṣipuruṣe paramātmani ceśvare |
nairāśye baṃdhamokṣe ca na ciṃtā muktaye mama || 14-3 ||

aṃtarvikalpaśūnyasya bahiḥ svacchandacāriṇaḥ |
bhrāntasyeva daśāstāstādṛśā eva jānate || 14-4 ||

14
Tranquillity

Janaka said:

14.1 He who by nature is empty minded, and who thinks of things only unintentionally, is freed from deliberate remembering like one awakened from a dream.

14.2 When my desire has been eliminated, I have no wealth, friends, robber senses, scriptures or knowledge?

14.3 Realizing my supreme self-nature in the Person of the Witness, the Lord, and the state of desirelessness in bondage or liberation, I feel no inclination for liberation.

14.4 The various states of one who is empty of uncertainty within, and who outwardly wanders about as he pleases like a madman, can only be known by someone in the same condition.

15

Tattvam

Aṣṭāvakra uvāca ||

yathātathopadeśena kṛtārthaḥ sattvabuddhimān |
ājīvamapi jijñāsuḥ parastatra vimuhyati || 15-1 ||

mokṣo viṣayavairasyaṃ bandho vaiṣayiko rasaḥ |
etāvadeva vijñānaṃ yathecchasi tathā kuru || 15-2 ||

vāgmiprājñāmahodyogaṃ janaṃ mūkajaḍālasam |
karoti tattvabodho'yamatastyakto bubhukṣabhiḥ || 15-3 ||

na tvaṃ deho na te deho bhoktā kartā na vā bhavān |
cidrūpo'si sadā sākṣī nirapekṣaḥ sukhaṃ cara || 15-4 ||

rāgadveṣau manodharmau na manaste kadācana |
nirvikalpo'si bodhātmā nirvikāraḥ sukhaṃ cara || 15-5 ||

sarvabhūteṣu cātmānaṃ sarvabhūtāni cātmani |
vijñāya nirahaṅkāro nirmamastvaṃ sukhī bhava || 15-6 ||

15
Knowledge of the Self

Aṣṭāvakra said:

15.1 While a man of pure intelligence may achieve the goal by the most casual of instruction, another may seek knowledge all his life and still remain bewildered.

15.2 Liberation is distaste for the objects of the senses. Bondage is love of the senses. This is knowledge. Now do as you please.

15.3 This awareness of the truth makes an eloquent, clever and energetic man dumb, stupid and lazy, so it is avoided by those whose aim is enjoyment.

15.4 You are not the body, nor is the body yours, nor are you the doer of actions or the reaper of their consequences. You are eternally pure consciousness the witness, in need of nothing—so live happily.

15.5 Desire and anger are objects of the mind, but the mind is not yours, nor ever has been. You are choiceless, awareness itself and unchanging—so live happily.

15.6 Recognizing oneself in all beings, and all beings in oneself, be happy, free from the sense of responsibility and free from preoccupation with "me".

viśvaṃ sphurati yatredaṃ taraṃgā iva sāgare |
tattvameva na sandehaścinmūrte vijvaro bhava || 15-7 ||

śraddhasva tāta śraddhasva nātra mo'haṃ kuruṣva bhoḥ |
jñānasvarūpo bhagavānātmā tvaṃ prakṛteḥ paraḥ || 15-8 ||

guṇaiḥ saṃveṣṭito dehastiṣṭhatyāyāti yāti ca |
ātmā na gaṃtā nāgaṃtā kimenamanuśocasi || 15-9 ||

dehastiṣṭhatu kalpāntaṃ gacchatvadyaiva vā punaḥ |
kva vṛddhiḥ kva ca vā hānistava cinmātrarūpiṇaḥ || 15-10 ||

tvayyanaṃtamahāmbhodhau viśvavīciḥ svabhāvataḥ |
udetu vāstamāyātu na te vṛddhirna vā kṣatiḥ || 15-11 ||

tāta cinmātrarūpo'si na te bhinnamidaṃ jagat |
ataḥ kasya kathaṃ kutra heyopādeyakalpanā || 15-12 ||

ekasminnavyaye śānte cidākāśe'male tvayi |
kuto janma kuto karma kuto'haṅkāra eva ca || 15-13 ||

yattvaṃ paśyasi tatraikastvameva pratibhāsase |
kiṃ pṛthak bhāsate svarṇāt kaṭakāṃgadanūpuram || 15-14 ||

15.7 Your nature is the consciousness, in which the whole world wells up, like waves in the sea. That is what you are, without any doubt, so be free of disturbance.

15.8 Have faith, my son, have faith. Don't let yourself be deluded in this, sir. You are yourself the Lord, whose property is knowledge, and are beyond natural causation.

15.9 The body invested with the senses stands still, and comes and goes. You yourself neither come nor go, so why bother about them?

15.10 Let the body last to the end of the Age, or let it come to an end right now. What have you gained or lost, who consist of pure consciousness?

15.11 Let the world wave rise or subside according to its own nature in you, the great ocean. It is no gain or loss to you.

15.12 My son, you consist of pure consciousness, and the world is not separate from you. So who is to accept or reject it, and how, and why?

15.13 How can there be either birth, karma or responsibility in that one unchanging, peaceful, unblemished and infinite consciousness which is you?

15.14 Whatever you see, it is you alone manifest in it. How could bracelets, armlets and anklets be different from the gold?

ayaṃ so'hamayaṃ nāhaṃ vibhāgamiti saṃtyaja |
sarvamātmeti niścitya niḥsaṅkalpaḥ sukhī bhava || 15-15 ||

tavaivājñānato viśvaṃ tvamekaḥ paramārthataḥ |
tvatto'nyo nāsti saṃsārī nāsaṃsārī ca kaścana || 15-16 ||

bhrāntimātramidaṃ viśvaṃ na kiṃciditi niścayī |
nirvāsanaḥ sphūrtimātro na kiṃcidiva śāmyati || 15-17 ||

eka eva bhavāmbhodhāvāsīdasti bhaviṣyati |
na te bandho'sti mokṣo vā kṛtyakṛtyaḥ sukhaṃ cara || 15-18 ||

mā saṅkalpavikalpābhyāṃ cittaṃ kṣobhaya cinmaya |
upaśāmya sukhaṃ tiṣṭha svātmanyānandavigrahe || 15-19 ||

tyajaiva dhyānaṃ sarvatra mā kiṃcid hṛdi dhāraya |
ātmā tvaṃ mukta evāsi kiṃ vimṛśya kariṣyasi || 15-20 ||

15.15 Giving up such distinctions as "This is what I am", and "I am not that", recognize that "Everything is myself", and be without distinction and happy.

15.16 It is through your ignorance that all this exists. In reality you alone exist. Apart from you there is no one within or beyond samsara.

15.17 Knowing that all this is an illusion, one becomes free from desire, pure receptivity and at peace, as if nothing existed.

15.18 Only one thing has existed, exists and will exist in the ocean of being. You have no bondage or liberation. Live happily and fulfilled.

15.19 Being pure consciousness, do not disturb your mind with thoughts of for and against. Be at peace and remain happily in yourself, the essence of joy.

15.20 Give up the practice of concentration completely and hold nothing in your mind. You are free in your very nature, so what will you achieve by working your brain?

16
Svāsthya

Aṣṭāvakra uvāca ||

ācakṣva śṛṇu vā tāta nānāśāstrāṇyanekaśaḥ |
tathāpi na tava svāsthyaṃ sarvavismaraṇād ṛte || 16-1 ||

bhogaṃ karma samādhiṃ vā kuru vijña tathāpi te |
cittaṃ nirastasarvāśamatyarthaṃ rocayiṣyati || 16-2 ||

āyāsātsakalo duḥkhī nainaṃ jānāti kaścana |
anenaivopadeśena dhanyaḥ prāpnoti nirvṛtim || 16-3 ||

vyāpāre khidyate yastu nimeṣonmeṣayorapi |
tasyālasya dhurīṇasya sukhaṃ nanyasya kasyacit || 16-4 ||

idaṃ kṛtamidaṃ neti dvaṃdvairmuktaṃ yadā manaḥ |
dharmārthakāmamokṣeṣu nirapekṣaṃ tadā bhavet || 16-5 ||

virakto viṣayadveṣṭā rāgī viṣayalolupaḥ |
grahamokṣavihīnastu na virakto na rāgavān || 16-6 ||

16
Special Instruction

Aṣṭāvakra said:

16.1 My son, you may recite or listen to countless scriptures, but you will not be established within until you can forget everything.

16.2 You may, as a learned man, indulge in wealth, activity and meditation, but your mind will still long for that which is the cessation of desire, and beyond all goals.

16.3 It is because of effort that everyone is in pain, but no-one realizes it. By just this simple instruction, the lucky one attains tranquility.

16.4 Happiness belongs to no-one but that supremely lazy man for whom even opening and closing his eyes is a bother.

16.5 When the mind is freed from such pairs of opposites as, "I have done this", and "I have not done that", it becomes indifferent to merit, wealth, sensuality and liberation.

16.6 One man is abstemious and averse to the senses, another is greedy and attached to them, but he who is free from both taking and rejecting is neither abstemious nor greedy.

heyopādeyatā tāvatsaṃsāraviṭapāṃkuraḥ |
spṛhā jīvati yāvad vai nirvicāradaśāspadam || 16-7 ||

pravṛttau jāyate rāgo nirvṛttau dveṣa eva hi |
nirdvandvo bālavad dhīmān evameva vyavasthitaḥ || 16-8 ||

hātumicchati saṃsāraṃ rāgī duḥkhajihāsayā |
vītarāgo hi nirduḥkhastasminnapi na khidyati || 16-9 ||

yasyābhimāno mokṣe'pi dehe'pi mamatā tathā |
na ca jñānī na vā yogī kevalaṃ duḥkhabhāgasau || 16-10 ||

haro yadyupadeṣṭā te hariḥ kamalajo'pi vā |
tathāpi na tava svāthyaṃ sarvavismaraṇādṛte || 16-11 ||

16.7 So long as desire, which is the state of lack of discrimination, remains, the sense of revulsion and attraction will remain, which is the root and branch of samsara.

16.8 Desire springs from usage, and aversion from abstention, but the wise man is free from the pairs of opposites like a child, and becomes established.

16.9 The passionate man wants to be rid of samsara so as to avoid pain, but the dispassionate man is without pain and feels no distress even in it.

16.10 He who is proud about even liberation or his own body, and feels them his own, is neither a seer or a yogi. He is still just a sufferer.

16.11 If even Shiva, Vishnu or the lotus-born Brahma were your instructor, until you have forgotten everything you cannot be established within.

17
Kaivalya

Aṣṭāvakra uvāca ||

tena jñānaphalaṃ prāptaṃ yogābhyāsaphalaṃ tathā |
tṛptaḥ svacchendriyo nityaṃ ekākī ramate tu yaḥ || 17-1 ||

na kadācijjagatyasmin tattvajño hanta khidyati |
yata ekena tenedaṃ pūrṇaṃ brahmāṇḍamaṇḍalam || 17-2 ||

na jātu viṣayāḥ ke'pi svārāmaṃ harṣayantyamī |
sallakīpallavaprītamivebhaṃ nimbapallavāḥ || 17-3 ||

yastu bhogeṣu bhukteṣu na bhavatyadhivāsitaḥ |
abhukteṣu nirākāṃkṣī tadṛśo bhavadurlabhaḥ || 17-4 ||

bubhukṣuriha saṃsāre mumukṣurapi dṛśyate |
bhogamokṣanirākāṃkṣī viralo hi mahāśayaḥ || 17-5 ||

dharmārthakāmamokṣeṣu jīvite maraṇe tathā |
kasyāpyudāracittasya heyopādeyatā na hi || 17-6 ||

17
The True Knower

Aṣṭāvakra said:

17.1 He who is content, with purified senses, and always enjoys solitude, has gained the fruit of knowledge and the fruit of the practice of yoga too.

17.2 The knower of truth is never distressed in this world, for the whole round world is full of himself alone.

17.3 None of these senses please a man who has found satisfaction within, just as Nimba leaves do not please the elephant that has a taste for Sallaki leaves.

17.4 Not attached to the things he has enjoyed, and not hankering after the things he has not enjoyed, such a man is hard to find.

17.5 Those who desire pleasure and those who desire liberation are both found in samsara, but the great souled man who desires neither pleasure nor liberation is rare indeed.

17.6 It is only the noble minded who is free from attraction or repulsion to religion, wealth, sensuality, and life and death too.

vāñchā na viśvavilaye na dveṣastasya ca sthitau |
yathā jīvikayā tasmād dhanya āste yathā sukham || 17-7 ||

kṛtārtho'nena jñānenetyevaṃ galitadhīḥ kṛtī |
paśyan śṛṇvan spṛśan jighrann
aśnannāste yathā sukham || 17-8 ||

śūnyā dṛṣṭirvṛthā ceṣṭā vikalānīndriyāṇi ca |
na spṛhā na viraktirvā kṣīṇasaṃsārasāgare || 17-9 ||

na jāgarti na nidrāti nonmīlati na mīlati |
aho paradaśā kvāpi vartate muktacetasaḥ || 17-10 ||

sarvatra dṛśyate svasthaḥ sarvatra vimalāśayaḥ |
samastavāsanā mukto muktaḥ sarvatra rājate || 17-11 ||

paśyan śṛṇvan spṛśan jighrann aśnan gṛṇhan vadan vrajan |
īhitānīhitairmukto mukta eva mahāśayaḥ || 17-12 ||

na nindati na ca stauti na hṛṣyati na kupyati |
na dadāti na gṛṇhāti muktaḥ sarvatra nīrasaḥ || 17-13 ||

sānurāgāṃ striyaṃ dṛṣṭvā mṛtyuṃ vā samupasthitam |
avihvalamanāḥ svastho mukta eva mahāśayaḥ || 17-14 ||

17.7 He feels no desire for the elimination of all this, nor anger at its continuing, so the lucky man lives happily with whatever means of sustenance presents itself.

17.8 Thus fulfilled through this knowledge, contented and with the thinking mind emptied, he lives happily just seeing, hearing, feeling, smelling and tasting.

17.9 In him for whom the ocean of samsara has dried up, there is neither attachment or aversion. His gaze is vacant, his behaviour purposeless, and his senses inactive.

17.10 Surely the supreme state is everywhere for the liberated mind. He is neither awake or asleep, and neither opens or closes his eyes.

17.11 The liberated man is resplendent everywhere, free from all desires. Everywhere he appears self-possessed and pure of heart.

17.12 Seeing, hearing, feeling, smelling, tasting, speaking and walking about, the great souled man who is freed from trying to achieve or avoid anything is free indeed.

17.13 The liberated man is free from desires everywhere. He does not blame, does not praise, does not rejoice, is not disappointed, and neither gives nor takes.

17.14 When a great souled one is equally unperturbed in mind and self-possessed at the sight of a woman full of desire and at approaching death, he is truly liberated.

sukhe duḥkhe nare nāryāṃ sampatsu ca vipatsu ca |
viśeṣo naiva dhīrasya sarvatra samadarśinaḥ || 17-15 ||

na hiṃsā naiva kāruṇyaṃ nauddhatyaṃ na ca dīnatā |
nāścaryaṃ naiva ca kṣobhaḥ kṣīṇasaṃsaraṇe nare || 17-16 ||

na mukto viṣayadveṣṭā na vā viṣayalolupaḥ |
asaṃsaktamanā nityaṃ prāptāprāptamupāśnute || 17-17 ||

samādhānasamādhānahitāhitavikalpanāḥ |
śūnyacitto na jānāti kaivalyamiva saṃsthitaḥ || 17-18 ||

nirmamo nirahaṃkāro na kiṃciditi niścitaḥ |
antargalitasarvāśaḥ kurvannapi karoti na || 17-19 ||

manaḥprakāśasaṃmohasvapnajāḍyavivarjitaḥ |
daśāṃ kāmapi samprāpto bhaved galitamānasaḥ || 17-20 ||

17.15 There is no distinction between pleasure and pain, man and woman, success and failure for the wise man who looks on everything as equal.

17.16 There is no aggression or compassion, no pride or humility, no wonder or confusion for the man whose days of running about are over.

17.17 The liberated man is not averse to the senses and nor is he attached to them. He enjoys himself continually with an unattached mind in both achievement and non-achievement.

17.18 One established in the Absolute state with an empty mind does not know the alternatives of inner stillness and lack of stillness, and of good and evil.

17.19 Free of "me" and "mine" and of a sense of responsibility, aware that "Nothing exists", with all desires extinguished within, a man does not act even in acting.

17.20 He whose thinking mind is dissolved achieves the indescribable state and is free from the mental display of delusion, dream and ignorance.

18

Jīvanmukti

Aṣṭāvakra uvāca ||

yasya bodhodaye tāvatsvapnavad bhavati bhramaḥ |
tasmai sukhaikarūpāya namaḥ śāntāya tejase || 18-1 ||

arjayitvākhilān arthān bhogānāpnoti puṣkalān |
na hi sarvaparityāgamantareṇa sukhī bhavet || 18-2 ||

kartavyaduḥkhamārtaṇḍajvālādagdhāntarātmanaḥ |
kutaḥ praśamapīyūṣadhārāsāramṛte sukham || 18-3 ||

bhavo'yaṃ bhāvanāmātro na kiṃcit paramarthataḥ |
nāstyabhāvaḥ svabhāvānāṃ bhāvābhāvavibhāvinām || 18-4 ||

na dūraṃ na ca saṃkocāllabdhamevātmanaḥ padam |
nirvikalpaṃ nirāyāsaṃ nirvikāraṃ niraṃjanam || 18-5 ||

vyāmohamātraviratau svarūpādānamātrataḥ |
vītaśokā virājante nirāvaraṇadṛṣṭayaḥ || 18-6 ||

18
Peace

Aṣṭāvakra said:

18.1 Praise be to that by the awareness of which delusion itself becomes dream-like, to that which is pure happiness, peace and light.

18.2 One may get all sorts of pleasure by the acquisition of various objects of enjoyment, but one cannot be happy except by the renunciation of everything.

18.3 How can there be happiness, for one who is burnt inside by the blistering sun of the pain of things that need doing, without the rain of the nectar of peace?

18.4 This existence is just imagination. It is nothing in reality, but there is no non-being for natures that know how to distinguish being from non being.

18.5 The realm of one's own self is not far away, and nor can it be achieved by the addition of limitations to its nature. It is unimaginable, effortless, unchanging and spotless.

18.6 By the simple elimination of delusion and the recognition of one's true nature, those whose vision is unclouded live free from sorrow.

samastaṃ kalpanāmātramātmā muktaḥ sanātanaḥ |
iti vijñāya dhīro hi kimabhyasyati bālavat || 18-7 ||

ātmā brahmeti niścitya bhāvābhāvau ca kalpitau |
niṣkāmaḥ kiṃ vijānāti kiṃ brūte ca karoti kim || 18-8 ||

ayaṃ so'hamayaṃ nāhaṃ iti kṣīṇā vikalpanā |
sarvamātmeti niścitya tūṣṇīmbhūtasya yoginaḥ || 18-9 ||

na vikṣepo na caikāgryaṃ nātibodho na mūḍhatā |
na sukhaṃ na ca vā duḥkhaṃ upaśāntasya yoginaḥ || 18-10 ||

svārājye bhaikṣavṛttau ca lābhālābhe jane vane |
nirvikalpasvabhāvasya na viśeṣo'sti yoginaḥ || 18-11 ||

kva dharmaḥ kva ca vā kāmaḥ kva cārthaḥ kva vivekitā |
idaṃ kṛtamidaṃ neti dvandvairmuktasya yoginaḥ || 18-12 ||

kṛtyaṃ kimapi naivāsti na kāpi hṛdi raṃjanā |
yathā jīvanameveha jīvanmuktasya yoginaḥ || 18-13 ||

kva mohaḥ kva ca vā viśvaṃ kva tad dhyānaṃ kva muktatā |
sarvasaṃkalpasīmāyāṃ viśrāntasya mahātmanaḥ || 18-14 ||

18.7 Knowing everything as just imagination, and himself as eternally free, how should the wise man behave like a fool?

18.8 Knowing himself to be God and being and non-being just imagination, what should the man free from desire learn, say or do?

18.9 Considerations like "I am this" or "I am not this" are finished for the yogi who has gone silent realizing "Everything is myself".

18.10 For the yogi who has found peace, there is no distraction or one-pointedness, no higher knowledge or ignorance, no pleasure and no pain.

18.11 The dominion of heaven or beggary, gain or loss, life among men or in the forest, these make no difference to a yogi whose nature it is to be free from distinctions.

18.12 There is no religion, wealth, sensuality or discrimination for a yogi free from the pairs of opposites such as "I have done this" and "I have not done that".

18.13 There is nothing needing to be done, or any attachment in his heart for the yogi liberated while still alive. Things are just for a life-time.

18.14 There is no delusion, world, meditation on That, or liberation for the pacified great soul. All these things are just the realm of imagination.

yena viśvamidaṃ dṛṣṭaṃ sa nāstīti karotu vai |
nirvāsanaḥ kiṃ kurute paśyannapi na paśyati || 18-15 ||

yena dṛṣṭaṃ paraṃ brahma so'haṃ brahmeti cintayet |
kiṃ cintayati niścinto dvitīyaṃ yo na paśyati || 18-16 ||

dṛṣṭo yenātmavikṣepo nirodhaṃ kurute tvasau |
udārastu na vikṣiptaḥ sādhyābhāvātkaroti kim || 18-17 ||

dhīro lokaviparyasto vartamāno'pi lokavat |
na samādhiṃ na vikṣepaṃ na lopaṃ svasya paśyati || 18-18 ||

bhāvābhāvavihīno yastṛpto nirvāsano budhaḥ |
naiva kiṃcitkṛtaṃ tena lokadṛṣṭyā vikurvatā || 18-19 ||

pravṛttau vā nivṛttau vā naiva dhīrasya durgrahaḥ |
yadā yatkartumāyāti tatkṛtvā tiṣṭhataḥ sukham || 18-20 ||

nirvāsano nirālambaḥ svacchando muktabandhanaḥ |
kṣiptaḥ saṃskāravātena ceṣṭate śuṣkaparṇavat || 18-21 ||

asaṃsārasya tu kvāpi na harṣo na viṣādatā |
sa śītalamanā nityaṃ videha iva rājaye || 18-22 ||

kutrāpi na jihāsāsti nāśo vāpi na kutracit |
ātmārāmasya dhīrasya śītalācchatarātmanaḥ || 18-23 ||

18.15 He by whom all this is seen may well make out he doesn't exist, but what is the desireless one to do? Even in seeing he does not see.

18.16 He by whom the Supreme Brahma is seen may think "I am Brahma", but what is he to think who is without thought, and who sees no duality.

18.17 He by whom inner distraction is seen may put an end to it, but the noble one is not distracted. When there is nothing to achieve, what is he to do?

18.18 The wise man, unlike the worldly man, does not see inner stillness, distraction or fault in himself, even when living like a worldly man.

18.19 Nothing is done by him who is free from being and non-being, who is contented, desireless and wise, even if in the world's eyes he does act.

18.20 The wise man who just goes on doing what presents itself for him to do, encounters no difficulty in either activity or inactivity.

18.21 He who is desireless, self-reliant, independent and free of bonds functions like a dead leaf blown about by the wind of causality.

18.22 There is neither joy nor sorrow for one who has transcended samsara. He lives always with a peaceful mind and as if without a body.

18.23 He whose joy is in himself, and who is peaceful and pure within has no desire for renunciation or sense of loss in anything.

prakṛtyā śūnyacittasya kurvato'sya yadṛcchayā |
prākṛtasyeva dhīrasya na māno nāvamānatā || 18-24 ||

kṛtaṃ dehena karmedaṃ na mayā śuddharūpiṇā |
iti cintānurodhī yaḥ kurvannapi karoti na || 18-25 ||

atadvādīva kurute na bhavedapi bāliśaḥ |
jīvanmuktaḥ sukhī śrīmān saṃsarannapi śobhate || 18-26 ||

nānāvicārasuśrānto dhīro viśrāntimāgataḥ |
na kalpate na jāti na śṛṇoti na paśyati || 18-27 ||

asamādheravikṣepān na mumukṣurna cetaraḥ |
niścitya kalpitaṃ paśyan brahmaivāste mahāśayaḥ || 18-28 ||

yasyāntaḥ syādahaṃkāro na karoti karoti saḥ |
nirahaṃkāradhīreṇa na kiṃcidakṛtaṃ kṛtam || 18-29 ||

nodvignaṃ na ca santuṣṭamakartṛ spandavarjitam |
nirāśaṃ gatasandehaṃ cittaṃ muktasya rājate || 18-30 ||

nirdhyātuṃ ceṣṭituṃ vāpi yaccittaṃ na pravartate |
nirnimittamidaṃ kiṃtu nirdhyāyeti viceṣṭate || 18-31 ||

tattvaṃ yathārthamākarṇya mandaḥ prāpnoti mūḍhatām |
athavā yāti saṃkocamamūḍhaḥ ko'pi mūḍhavat || 18-32 ||

18.24 For the man with a naturally empty mind, doing just as he pleases, there is no such thing as pride or false humility, as there is for the natural man.

18.25 "This action was done by the body but not by me". The pure-natured person thinking like this, is not acting even when acting.

18.26 He who acts without being able to say why, but not because he is a fool, he is one liberated while still alive, happy and blessed. He thrives even in samsara.

18.27 He who has had enough of endless considerations and has attained to peace, does not think, know, hear or see.

18.28 He who is beyond mental stillness and distraction, does not desire either liberation or anything else. Recognizing that things are just constructions of the imagination, that great soul lives as God here and now.

18.29 He who feels responsibility within, acts even when not acting, but there is no sense of done or undone for the wise man who is free from the sense of responsibility.

18.30 The mind of the liberated man is not upset or pleased. It shines unmoving, desireless, and free from doubt.

18.31 He whose mind does not set out to meditate or act, meditates and acts without an object.

18.32 A stupid man is bewildered when he hears the real truth, while even a clever man is humbled by it just like the fool.

ekāgratā nirodho vā mūḍhairabhyasyate bhṛśam |
dhīrāḥ kṛtyaṃ na paśyanti suptavatsvapade sthitāḥ || 18-33 ||

aprayatnāt prayatnād vā mūḍho nāpnoti nirvṛtim |
tattvaniścayamātreṇa prājño bhavati nirvṛtaḥ || 18-34 ||

śuddhaṃ buddhaṃ priyaṃ pūrṇaṃ niṣprapaṃcaṃ nirāmayam |
ātmānaṃ taṃ na jānanti tatrābhyāsaparā janāḥ || 18-35 ||

nāpnoti karmaṇā mokṣaṃ vimūḍho'bhyāsarūpiṇā |
dhanyo vijñānamātreṇa muktastiṣṭhatyavikriyaḥ || 18-36 ||

mūḍho nāpnoti tad brahma yato bhavitumicchati |
anicchannapi dhīro hi parabrahmasvarūpabhāk || 18-37 ||

nirādhārā grahavyagrā mūḍhāḥ saṃsārapoṣakāḥ |
etasyānarthamūlasya mūlacchedaḥ kṛto budhaiḥ || 18-38 ||

na śāntiṃ labhate mūḍho yataḥ śamitumicchati |
dhīrastattvaṃ viniścitya sarvadā śāntamānasaḥ || 18-39 ||

kvātmano darśanaṃ tasya yad dṛṣṭamavalambate |
dhīrāstaṃ taṃ na paśyanti paśyantyātmānamavyayam || 18-40 ||

18.33 The ignorant make a great effort to practise one-pointedness and the stopping of thought, while the wise see nothing to be done and remain in themselves like those asleep.

18.34 The stupid does not attain cessation whether he acts or abandons action, while the wise man find peace within simply by knowing the truth.

18.35 People cannot come to know themselves by practices—pure awareness, clear, complete, beyond multiplicity and faultless though they are.

18.36 The stupid does not achieve liberation even through regular practice, but the fortunate remains free and actionless simply by discrimination.

18.37 The stupid does not attain Godhead because he wants to become it, while the wise man enjoys the Supreme Godhead without even wanting it.

18.38 Even when living without any support and eager for achievement, the stupid are still nourishing samsara, while the wise have cut at the very root of its unhappiness.

18.39 The stupid does not find peace because he is wanting it, while the wise discriminating the truth is always peaceful minded. 18.39

18.40 How can there be self knowledge for him whose knowledge depends on what he sees. The wise do not see this and that, but see themselves as unending.

kva nirodho vimūḍhasya yo nirbandhaṃ karoti vai |
svārāmasyaiva dhīrasya sarvadāsāvakṛtrimaḥ || 18-41 ||

bhāvasya bhāvakaḥ kaścin na kiṃcid bhāvakoparaḥ |
ubhayābhāvakaḥ kaścid evameva nirākulaḥ || 18-42 ||

śuddhamadvayamātmānaṃ bhāvayanti kubuddhayaḥ |
na tu jānanti saṃmohādyāvajjīvamanirvṛtāḥ || 18-43 ||

mumukṣorbuddhirālambamantareṇa na vidyate |
nirālambaiva niṣkāmā buddhirmuktasya sarvadā || 18-44 ||

viṣayadvīpino vīkṣya cakitāḥ śaraṇārthinaḥ |
viśanti jhaṭiti kroḍaṃ nirodhaikāgrasiddhaye || 18-45 ||

nirvāsanaṃ hariṃ dṛṣṭvā tūṣṇīṃ viṣayadantinaḥ |
palāyante na śaktāste sevante kṛtacāṭavaḥ || 18-46 ||

na muktikārikāṃ dhatte niḥśaṅko yuktamānasaḥ |
paśyan śṛṇvan spṛśan jighrannaśnannāste yathāsukham || 18-47 ||

vastuśravaṇamātreṇa śuddhabuddhirnirākulaḥ |
naivācāramanācāramaudāsyaṃ vā prapaśyati || 18-48 ||

18.41 How can there be cessation of thought for the misguided who is striving for it. Yet it is there always naturally for the wise man delighted in himself.

18.42 Some think that something exists, and others that nothing does. Rare is the man who does not think either, and is thereby free from distraction.

18.43 Those of weak intelligence think of themselves as pure nonduality, but because of their delusion do not know this, and remain unfulfilled all their lives.

18.44 The mind of the man seeking liberation can find no resting place within, but the mind of the liberated man is always free from desire by the very fact of being without a resting place.

18.45 Seeing the tigers of the senses, the frightened refuge-seekers at once enter the cave in search of cessation of thought and one-pointedness.

18.46 Seeing the desireless lion the elephants of the senses silently run away, or, if they cannot, serve him like courtiers.

18.47 The man who is free from doubts and whose mind is free does not bother about means of liberation. Whether seeing, hearing, feeling smelling or tasting, he lives at ease.

18.48 He whose mind is pure and undistracted from the simple hearing of the Truth sees neither something to do nor something to avoid nor a cause for indifference.

yadā yatkartumāyāti tadā tatkurute ṛjuḥ |
śubhaṃ vāpyaśubhaṃ vāpi tasya ceṣṭā hi bālavat || 18-49 ||

svātaṃtryātsukhamāpnoti svātaṃtryāllabhate param |
svātaṃtryānnirvṛtiṃ gacchetsvātaṃtryāt paramaṃ padam || 18-50 ||

akartṛtvamabhoktṛtvaṃ svātmano manyate yadā |
tadā kṣīṇā bhavantyeva samastāścittavṛttayaḥ || 18-51 ||

ucchṛṃkhalāpyakṛtikā sthitirdhīrasya rājate |
na tu saspṛhacittasya śāntirmūḍhasya kṛtrimā || 18-52 ||

vilasanti mahābhogairviśanti girigahvarān |
nirastakalpanā dhīrā abaddhā muktabuddhayaḥ || 18-53 ||

śrotriyaṃ devatāṃ tīrthamaṅganāṃ bhūpatiṃ priyam |
dṛṣṭvā sampūjya dhīrasya na kāpi hṛdi vāsanā || 18-54 ||

bhṛtyaiḥ putraiḥ kalatraiśca dauhitraiścāpi gotrajaiḥ |
vihasya dhikkṛto yogī na yāti vikṛtiṃ manāk || 18-55 ||

santuṣṭo'pi na santuṣṭaḥ khinno'pi na ca khidyate |
tasyāścaryadaśāṃ tāṃ tāṃ tādṛśā eva jānate || 18-56 ||

kartavyataiva saṃsāro na tāṃ paśyanti sūrayaḥ |
śūnyākārā nirākārā nirvikārā nirāmayāḥ || 18-57 ||

18.49 The straightforward person does whatever arrives to be done, good or bad, for his actions are like those of a child.

18.50 By inner freedom one attains happiness, by inner freedom one reaches the Supreme, by inner freedom one comes to absence of thought, by inner freedom to the Ultimate State.

18.51 When one sees oneself as neither the doer nor the reaper of the consequences, then all mind waves come to an end.

18.52 The spontaneous unassumed behaviour of the wise is noteworthy, but not the deliberate, intentional stillness of the fool.

18.53 The wise who are rid of imagination, unbound and with unfettered awareness may enjoy themselves in the midst of many goods, or alternatively go off to mountain caves.

18.54 There is no attachment in the heart of a wise man whether he sees or pays homage to a learned brahmin, a celestial being, a holy place, a woman, a king or a friend.

18.55 A yogi is not in the least put out even when humiliated by the ridicule of servants, sons, wives, grandchildren or other relatives.

18.56 Even when pleased he is not pleased, not suffering even when in pain. Only those like him can know the wonderful state of such a man.

18.57 It is the sense of responsibility which is samsara. The wise who are of the form of emptiness, formless, unchanging and spotless see no such thing.

akurvannapi saṅkṣobhād vyagraḥ sarvatra mūḍhadhīḥ |
kurvannapi tu kṛtyāni kuśalo hi nirākulaḥ || 18-58 ||

sukhamāste sukhaṃ śete sukhamāyāti yāti ca |
sukhaṃ vakti sukhaṃ bhuṃkte vyavahāre'pi śāntadhīḥ || 18-59 ||

svabhāvādyasya naivārtirlokavad vyavahāriṇaḥ |
mahāhṛda ivākṣobhyo gatakleśaḥ suśobhate || 18-60 ||

nivṛttirapi mūḍhasya pravṛtti rupajāyate |
pravṛttirapi dhīrasya nivṛttiphalabhāginī || 18-61 ||

parigraheṣu vairāgyaṃ prāyo mūḍhasya dṛśyate |
dehe vigalitāśasya kva rāgaḥ kva virāgatā || 18-62 ||

bhāvanābhāvanāsaktā dṛṣṭirmūḍhasya sarvadā |
bhāvyabhāvanayā sā tu svasthasyādṛṣṭirūpiṇī || 18-63 ||

sarvārambheṣu niṣkāmo yaścared bālavan muniḥ |
na lepastasya śuddhasya kriyamāṇe'pi karmaṇi || 18-64 ||

sa eva dhanya ātmajñaḥ sarvabhāveṣu yaḥ samaḥ |
paśyan śṛṇvan spṛśan jighrann aśnannistarṣamānasaḥ || 18-65 ||

18.58 Even when doing nothing the fool is agitated by restlessness, while a skilful man remains undisturbed even when doing what there is to do.

18.59 Happy he stands, happy he sits, happy sleeps and happy he comes and goes. Happy he speaks, and happy he eats. Such is the life of a man at peace.

18.60 He who of his very nature feels no unhappiness in his daily life like worldly people, remains undisturbed like a great lake, all sorrow gone.

18.61 Even abstention from action leads to action in a fool, while even the action of the wise man brings the fruits of inaction.

18.62 A fool often shows aversion towards his belongings, but for him whose attachment to the body has dropped away, there is neither attachment nor aversion.

18.63 The mind of the fool is always caught in an opinion about becoming or avoiding something, but the wise man's nature is to have no opinions about becoming and avoiding.

18.64 For the seer who behaves like a child, without desire in all actions, there is no attachment for such a pure one even in the work he does.

18.65 Blessed is he who knows himself and is the same in all states, with a mind free from craving whether he is seeing, hearing, feeling, smelling or tasting.

kva saṃsāraḥ kva cābhāsaḥ kva sādhyaṃ kva ca sādhanam |
ākāśasyeva dhīrasya nirvikalpasya sarvadā || 18-66 ||

sa jayatyarthasaṃnyāsī pūrṇasvarasavigrahaḥ |
akṛtrimo'navacchinne samādhiryasya vartate || 18-67 ||

bahunātra kimuktena jñātatattvo mahāśayaḥ |
bhogamokṣanirākāṅkṣī sadā sarvatra nīrasaḥ || 18-68 ||

mahadādi jagaddvaitaṃ nāmamātravijṛmbhitam |
vihāya śuddhabodhasya kiṃ kṛtyamavaśiṣyate || 18-69 ||

bhramabhūtamidaṃ sarvaṃ kiṃcinnāstīti niścayī |
alakṣyasphuraṇaḥ śuddhaḥ svabhāvenaiva śāmyati || 18-70 ||

śuddhasphuraṇarūpasya dṛśyabhāvamapaśyataḥ |
kva vidhiḥ kva ca vairāgyaṃ kva tyāgaḥ kva śamo'pi vā || 18-71 ||

sphurato'nantarūpeṇa prakṛtiṃ ca na paśyataḥ |
kva bandhaḥ kva ca vā mokṣaḥ kva harṣaḥ kva viṣāditā || 18-72 ||

buddhiparyantasaṃsāre māyāmātraṃ vivartate |
nirmamo nirahaṃkāro niṣkāmaḥ śobhate budhaḥ || 18-73 ||

18.66 There is no man subject to samsara, sense of individuality, goal or means to the goal for the wise man who is always free from imaginations, and unchanging as space.

18.67 Glorious is he who has abandoned all goals and is the incarnation of satisfaction, his very nature, and whose inner focus on the Unconditioned is quite spontaneous.

18.68 In brief, the great-souled man who has come to know the Truth is without desire for either pleasure or liberation, and is always and everywhere free from attachment.

18.69 What remains to be done by the man who is pure awareness and has abandoned everything that can be expressed in words from the highest heaven to the earth itself?

18.70 The pure man who has experienced the Indescribable attains peace by his own nature, realizing that all this is nothing but illusion, and that nothing is.

18.71 There are no rules, dispassion, renunciation or meditation for one who is pure receptivity by nature, and admits no knowable form of being?

18.72 For him who shines with the radiance of Infinity and is not subject to natural causality there is neither bondage, liberation, pleasure nor pain.

18.73 Pure illusion reigns in samsara which will continue until self realization, but the enlightened man lives in the beauty of freedom from me and mine, from the sense of responsibility and from any attachment.

akṣayaṃ gatasantāpamātmānaṃ paśyato muneḥ |
kva vidyā ca kva vā viśvaṃ kva deho'haṃ mameti vā || 18-74 ||

nirodhādīni karmāṇi jahāti jaḍadhīryadi |
manorathān pralāpāṃśca kartumāpnotyatatkṣaṇāt || 18-75 ||

mandaḥ śrutvāpi tadvastu na jahāti vimūḍhatām |
nirvikalpo bahiryatnādantarviṣayalālasaḥ || 18-76 ||

jñānād galitakarmā yo lokadṛṣṭyāpi karmakṛt |
nāpnotyavasaraṃ kartruṃ vaktumeva na kiṃcana || 18-77 ||

kva tamaḥ kva prakāśo vā hānaṃ kva ca na kiṃcana |
nirvikārasya dhīrasya nirātaṃkasya sarvadā || 18-78 ||

kva dhairyaṃ kva vivekitvaṃ kva nirātaṃkatāpi vā |
anirvācyasvabhāvasya niḥsvabhāvasya yoginaḥ || 18-79 ||

na svargo naiva narako jīvanmuktirna caiva hi |
bahunātra kimuktena yogadṛṣṭyā na kiṃcana || 18-80 ||

naiva prārthayate lābhaṃ nālābhenānuśocati |
dhīrasya śītalaṃ cittamamṛtenaiva pūritam || 18-81 ||

na śāntaṃ stauti niṣkāmo na duṣṭamapi nindati |
samaduḥkhasukhastṛptaḥ kiṃcit kṛtyaṃ na paśyati || 18-82 ||

18.74 For the seer who knows himself as imperishable and beyond pain there is neither knowledge, a world nor the sense that I am the body or the body mine.

18.75 No sooner does a man of low intelligence give up activities like the elimination of thought than he falls into mental chariot racing and babble.

18.76 A fool does not get rid of his stupidity even on hearing the truth. He may appear outwardly free from imaginations, but inside he is hankering after the senses still.

18.77 Though in the eyes of the world he is active, the man who has shed action through knowledge finds no means of doing or speaking anything.

18.78 For the wise man who is always unchanging and fearless there is neither darkness nor light nor destruction, nor anything.

18.79 There is neither fortitude, prudence nor courage for the yogi whose nature is beyond description and free of individuality.

18.80 There is neither heaven nor hell nor even liberation during life. In a nutshell, in the sight of the seer nothing exists at all.

18.81 He neither longs for possessions nor grieves at their absence. The calm mind of the sage is full of the nectar of immortality.

18.82 The dispassionate does not praise the good or blame the wicked. Content and equal in pain and pleasure, he sees nothing that needs doing.

dhīro na dveṣṭi saṃsāramātmānaṃ na didṛkṣati |
harṣāmarṣavinirmukto na mṛto na ca jīvati || 18-83 ||

niḥsnehaḥ putradārādau niṣkāmo viṣayeṣu ca |
niścintaḥ svaśarīre'pi nirāśaḥ śobhate budhaḥ || 18-84 ||

tuṣṭiḥ sarvatra dhīrasya yathāpatitavartinaḥ |
svacchandaṃ carato deśān yatrastamitaśāyinaḥ || 18-85 ||

patatūdetu vā deho nāsya cintā mahātmanaḥ |
svabhāvabhūmiviśrāntivismṛtāśeṣasaṃsṛteḥ || 18-86 ||

akiṃcanaḥ kāmacāro nirdvandvaśchinnasaṃśayaḥ |
asaktaḥ sarvabhāveṣu kevalo ramate budhaḥ || 18-87 ||

nirmamaḥ śobhate dhīraḥ samaloṣṭāśmakāñcanaḥ |
subhinnahṛdayagranthirvinirdhūtarajastamaḥ || 18-88 ||

sarvatrānavadhānasya na kiṃcid vāsanā hṛdi |
muktātmano vitṛptasya tulanā kena jāyate || 18-89 ||

jānannapi na jānāti paśyannapi na paśyati |
bruvann api na ca brūte ko'nyo nirvāsanādṛte || 18-90 ||

18.83 The wise man does not dislike samsara or seek to know himself. Free from pleasure and impatience, he is not dead and he is not alive.

18.84 The wise man stands out by being free from anticipation, without attachment to such things as children or wives, free from desire for the senses, and not even concerned about his own body.

18.85 Peace is everywhere for the wise man who lives on whatever happens to come to him, going to wherever he feels like, and sleeping wherever the sun happens to set.

18.86 Let his body rise or fall. The great souled one gives it no thought, having forgotten all about samsara in coming to rest on the ground of his true nature.

18.87 The wise man has the joy of being complete in himself and without possessions, acting as he pleases, free from duality and rid of doubts, and without attachment to any creature.

18.88 The wise man excels in being without the sense of "me". Earth, a stone or gold are the same to him. The knots of his heart have been rent asunder, and he is freed from greed and blindness.

18.89 Who can compare with that contented, liberated soul who pays no regard to anything and has no desire left in his heart?

18.90 Who but the upright man without desire knows without knowing, sees without seeing and speaks without speaking?

bhikṣurvā bhūpatirvāpi yo niṣkāmaḥ sa śobhate |
bhāveṣu galitā yasya śobhanāśobhanā matiḥ || 18-91 ||

kva svācchandyaṃ kva saṃkocaḥ kva vā tattvaviniścayaḥ |
nirvyājārjavabhūtasya caritārthasya yoginaḥ || 18-92 ||

ātmaviśrāntitṛptena nirāśena gatārtinā |
antaryadanubhūyeta tat kathaṃ kasya kathyate || 18-93 ||

supto'pi na suṣuptau ca svapne'pi śayito na ca |
jāgare'pi na jāgarti dhīrastṛptaḥ pade pade || 18-94 ||

jñaḥ sacinto'pi niścintaḥ sendriyo'pi nirindriyaḥ |
subuddhirapi nirbuddhiḥ sāhaṃkāro'nahaṅkṛtiḥ || 18-95 ||

na sukhī na ca vā duḥkhī na virakto na saṃgavān |
na mumukṣurna vā muktā na kiṃcinnna ca kiṃcana || 18-96 ||

vikṣepe'pi na vikṣiptaḥ samādhau na samādhimān |
jāḍye'pi na jaḍo dhanyaḥ pāṇḍitye'pi na paṇḍitaḥ || 18-97 ||

mukto yathāsthitisvasthaḥ kṛtakartavyanirvṛtaḥ |
samaḥ sarvatra vaitṛṣṇyānna smaratyakṛtaṃ kṛtam || 18-98 ||

18.91 Beggar or king, he excels who is without desire, and whose opinion of things is rid of "good" and "bad".

18.92 There is neither dissolute behaviour nor virtue, nor even discrimination of the truth for the sage who has reached the goal and is the very embodiment of guileless sincerity.

18.93 How can one describe what is experienced within by one desireless and free from pain, and content to rest in himself—and of whom?

18.94 The wise man who is contented in all circumstances is not asleep even in deep sleep, not sleeping in a dream, nor waking when he is awake.

18.95 The seer is without thoughts even when thinking, without senses among the senses, without understanding even in understanding and without a sense of responsibility even in the ego.

18.96 Neither happy nor unhappy, neither detached nor attached, neither seeking liberation nor liberated, he is neither something nor nothing.

18.97 Not distracted in distraction, in mental stillness not poised, in stupidity not stupid, that blessed one is not even wise in his wisdom.

18.98 The liberated man is self-possessed in all circumstances and free from the idea of "done" and "still to do". He is the same wherever he is and without greed. He does not dwell on what he has done or not done.

na prīyate vandyamāno nindyamāno na kupyati |
naivodvijati maraṇe jīvane nābhinandati || 18-99 ||

na dhāvati janākīrṇaṃ nāraṇyaṃ upaśāntadhīḥ |
yathātathā yatratatra sama evāvatiṣṭhate || 18-100 ||

18.99 He is not pleased when praised nor upset when blamed. He is not afraid of death nor attached to life.

18.100 A man at peace does not run off to popular resorts or to the forest. Whatever and wherever, he remains the same.

19
Svamahimā

Janaka uvāca ||

tattvavijñānasandaṃśamādāya hṛdayodarāt |
nāvidhaparāmarśaśalyoddhāraḥ kṛto mayā || 19-1 ||

kva dharmaḥ kva ca vā kāmaḥ kva cārthaḥ kva vivekitā |
kva dvaitaṃ kva ca vā'dvaitaṃ svamahimni sthitasya me || 19-2 ||

kva bhūtaṃ kva bhaviṣyad vā vartamānamapi kva vā |
kva deśaḥ kva ca vā nityaṃ svamahimni sthitasya me || 19-3 ||

kva cātmā kva ca vānātmā kva śubhaṃ kvāśubhaṃ yathā |
kva cintā kva ca vācintā svamahimni sthitasya me || 19-4 ||

kva svapnaḥ kva suṣuptirvā kva ca jāgaraṇaṃ tathā |
kva turīyaṃ bhayaṃ vāpi svamahimni sthitasya me || 19-5 ||

kva dūraṃ kva samīpaṃ vā bāhyaṃ kvābhyantaraṃ kva vā |
kva sthūlaṃ kva ca vā sūkṣmaṃ svamahimni sthitasya me || 19-6 ||

19
Repose in the Self

Janaka said:

19.1 Using the tweezers of the knowledge of the truth I have managed to extract the painful thorn of endless opinions from the recesses of my heart.

19.2 For me, established in my own glory, there is no religion, sensuality, possessions, philosophy, duality or even non-duality.

19.3 For me established in my own glory, there is no past, future or present. There is no space or even eternity.

19.4 For me established in my own glory, there is no self or non-self, no good or evil, no thought or even absence of thought.

19.5 For me established in my own glory, there is no dreaming or deep sleep, no waking nor fourth state beyond them, and certainly no fear.

19.6 For me established in my own glory, there is nothing far away and nothing near, nothing within or without, nothing large and nothing small.

kva mṛtyurjīvitaṃ vā kva lokāḥ kvāsya kva laukikam |
kva layaḥ kva samādhirvā svamahimni sthitasya me || 19-7 ||

alaṃ trivargakathayā yogasya kathayāpyalam |
alaṃ vijñānakathayā viśrāntasya mamātmani || 19-8 ||

19.7 For me established in my own glory, there is no life or death, no worlds or things of the world, no distraction and no stillness of mind.

19.8 For me remaining in myself, there is no need for talk of the three goals of life, of yoga or of knowledge.

20

Akiñcanabhava

Janaka uvāca ||

kva bhūtāni kva deho vā kvendriyāṇi kva vā manaḥ |
kva śūnyaṃ kva ca nairāśyaṃ matsvarūpe niraṃjane || 20-1 ||

kva śāstraṃ kvātmavijñānaṃ kva vā nirviṣayaṃ manaḥ |
kva tṛptiḥ kva vitṛṣṇātvaṃ gatadvandvasya me sadā || 20-2 ||

kva vidyā kva ca vāvidyā kvāhaṃ kvedaṃ mama kva vā |
kva bandha kva ca vā mokṣaḥ svarūpasya kva rūpitā || 20-3 ||

kva prārabdhāni karmāṇi jīvanmuktirapi kva vā |
kva tad videhakaivalyaṃ nirviśeṣasya sarvadā || 20-4 ||

kva kartā kva ca vā bhoktā niṣkriyaṃ sphuraṇaṃ kva vā |
kvāparokṣaṃ phalaṃ vā kva niḥsvabhāvasya me sadā || 20-5 ||

kva lokaṃ kva mumukṣurvā kva yogī jñānavān kva vā |
kva baddhaḥ kva ca vā muktaḥ svasvarūpe'hamadvaye || 20-6 ||

20
Liberation-in-Life

Janaka said:

20.1 In my unblemished nature there are no elements, no body, no faculties, no mind. There is no void and no anguish.

20.2 For me, free from the sense of dualism, there are no scriptures, no self-knowledge, no mind free from an object, no satisfaction and no freedom from desire.

20.3 There is no knowledge or ignorance, no "me", "this" or "mine", no bondage, no liberation and no property of self-nature.

20.4 For him who is always free from individual characteristics there is no antecedent causal action, no liberation during life, and no fulfilment at death.

20.5 For me free from individuality, there is no doer and no reaper of the consequences, no cessation of action, no arising of thought, no immediate object, and no idea of results.

20.6 There is no world, no seeker for liberation, no yogi, no seer, no-one bound and no-one liberated. I remain in my own non-dual nature.

kva sṛṣṭiḥ kva ca saṃhāraḥ kva sādhyaṃ kva ca sādhanam |
kva sādhakaḥ kva siddhirvā svasvarūpe'hamadvaye || 20-7 ||

kva pramātā pramāṇaṃ vā kva prameyaṃ kva ca pramā |
kva kiṃcit kva na kiṃcid vā sarvadā vimalasya me || 20-8 ||

kva vikṣepaḥ kva caikāgryaṃ kva nirbodhaḥ kva mūḍhatā |
kva harṣaḥ kva viṣādo vā sarvadā niṣkriyasya me || 20-9 ||

kva caiṣa vyavahāro vā kva ca sā paramārthatā |
kva sukhaṃ kva ca vā dukhaṃ nirvimarśasya me sadā || 20-10 ||

kva māyā kva ca saṃsāraḥ kva prītirviratiḥ kva vā |
kva jīvaḥ kva ca tadbrahma sarvadā vimalasya me || 20-11 ||

kva pravṛttirnirvṛttirvā kva muktiḥ kva ca bandhanam |
kūṭasthanirvibhāgasya svasthasya mama sarvadā || 20-12 ||

kvopadeśaḥ kva vā śāstraṃ kva śiṣyaḥ kva ca vā guruḥ |
kva cāsti puruṣārtho vā nirupādheḥ śivasya me || 20-13 ||

kva cāsti kva ca vā nāsti kvāsti caikaṃ kva ca dvayam |
bahunātra kimuktena kiṃcinnottiṣṭhate mama || 20-14 ||

|| Oṁ tatsat ||

20.7 There is no emanation or return, no goal, means, seeker or achievement. I remain in my own non-dual nature.

20.8 For I am forever unblemished; there is no judge, no standard, nothing to judge, and no judgement.

20.9 For I am forever actionless; there is no distraction or one-pointedness of mind, no lack of understanding, no stupidity, no joy and no sorrow.

20.10 For I am always free from deliberations; there is neither conventional truth nor absolute truth, no happiness and no suffering.

20.11 For I am forever pure; there is no illusion, no samsara, no attachment or detachment, no living being and no God.

20.12 For I am forever immovable and indivisible, established in myself; there is no activity or inactivity, no liberation and no bondage.

20.13 For I am blessed and without limitation; there is no initiation or scripture, no disciple or teacher and no goal of human existence.

20.14 There is no being or non-being, no unity or dualism. What more is there to say? Nothing arises out of me.

www.ingramcontent.com/pod-product-compliance
Lightning Source LLC
Chambersburg PA
CBHW031651040426
42453CB00006B/269

* 9 7 8 1 7 8 2 0 1 2 6 1 0 *